The Grisly History of Medicine

Kill or Cure

STRANGE AND SCARY TREATMENTS

Thanks to the creative team:

Senior Editor: Alice Peebles

Editor: Angela Koo

Fact Checker: Kate Mitchell

Design: www.collaborate.agency

First published in Great Britain in 2016
by Hungry Tomato Ltd
PO Box 181
Edenbridge
Kent, TN8 9DP

A CIP catalogue record for this book is
available from the British Library.

ISBN 978-1-910684-64-1

Printed and bound in China

Discover more at
www.hungrytomato.com

The Grisly History of Medicine

Kill or Cure

By John Farndon
Illustrated by Venitia Dean

HUNGRY TOMATO.

Contents

Introduction   6

Cutting and Drilling   8

Old Doctors   10

Bad Moods   12

Body Butchers – the Anatomists   14

Leeches and Bloodletting   16

Barbers and Quacks   18

New Blood   20

Sick Hospitals   22

Taking the Pustule   24

Can't Feel a Thing   26

Medical Times   28

Doctors Make Me Sick!   30

Glossary   31

Index   32

INTRODUCTION

People have always got sick so they have always needed doctors. But while most doctors try to make you better, sometimes in the past their methods were weird, yucky or even dangerous. Did you know there were doctors who liked to drink your urine, and others that liked to blow smoke up your rear end? Well, read on...

Is there a doctor in the house?

There are between 10 and 15 million doctors in the world. People in Spain have more doctors each than anywhere else in the world. The World Health Organization thinks that we really need over 4 million more doctors.

Long training

If you want to be a doctor, you've a lot to learn! It takes ten years on average to train to be a general practitioner (GP). Some specialists have to train for up to 16 years before they are fully qualified.

Lady doctor?

There were women doctors as long ago as the time of Ancient Egypt. But they often had to pretend to be men to be allowed to practise, like Agnodice in Ancient Greece, and the British Army doctor, James Barry (Margaret Ann Bulkley), who lived in the 19th century.

There's money in medicine

In the USA, doctors are generally well paid. The best paid are specialists in orthopaedics, who treat bones and muscles. They earn nearly half a million dollars a year.

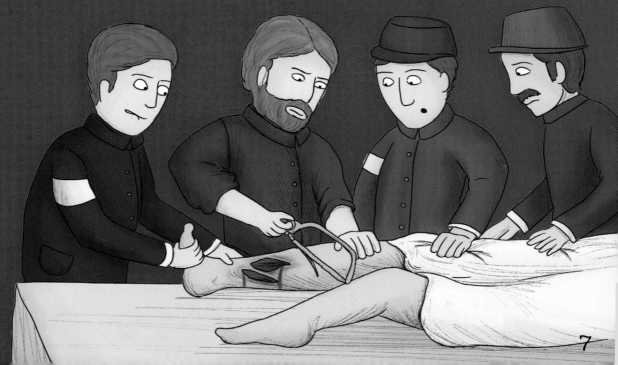

CUTTING AND DRILLING

Today surgery is done with the latest high tech equipment while you're asleep. But the first surgeons cut into you while you lay screaming in agony. Sometimes, though, they might just have saved your life.

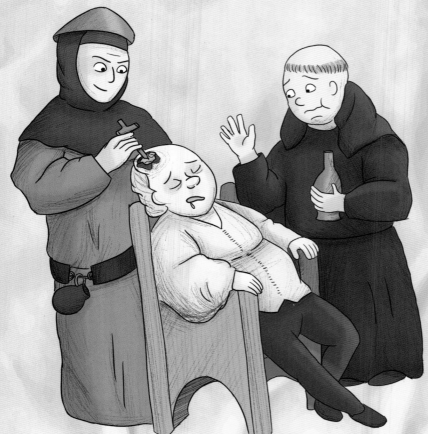

Hole in the head

'Trepanning' dates back at least 8,500 years. It involves drilling a large hole in the skull! It sounds unbelievably painful and very dangerous. Yet trepanning was practised right up until a few hundred years ago. No one really knows why. Maybe it was to stop people suffering fits, or to let evil spirits out.

Stitched up!

Surgeons were stitching up serious wounds with a needle and thread at least 6,000 years ago. They'd sew the wound together with a bone needle and thread made from animal tendons or plant fibres. Now we call this 'suturing'. Back then they probably just said 'aaagh'!

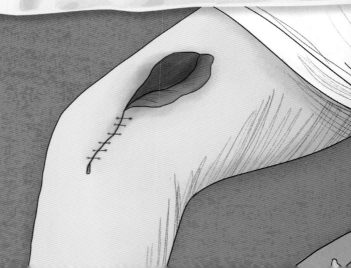

Nose job

In 15th-century Italy, if you lost your nose in a sword fight (as many did), you went to Dr Gaspare Tagliacozzi. Tagliacozzi would rebuild your nose for you by grafting skin from your arm. This meant going around with your arm sewn to your nose for months. And it wasn't guaranteed to work.

Nose job no. 2

The earliest known plastic surgeon, Sushruta, lived in India 2,800 years ago. Back then, noses were chopped off as a punishment. So Sushruta developed a line in rebuilding noses. He simply cut a flap from your cheek then folded it over to make a new nose, holding it in place with stitches until it was properly grafted (attached).

One black leg, one white

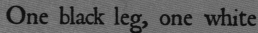

Back in the 3rd century, the leg of a church deacon in Constantinople became infected. No problem, said local saints Cosmas and Damian to the deacon, in a dream. They cut off his diseased leg and stitched another in its place, chopped from a newly dead body. But the dead man was black. So when the deacon woke up, he had one black leg and one white! If the story is true, it was the first ever transplant...

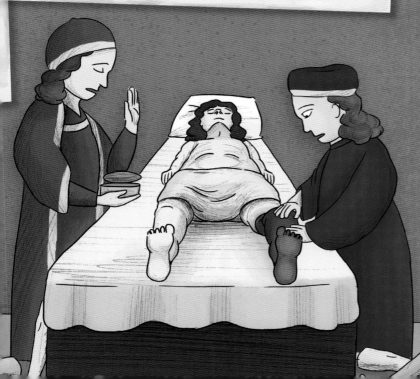

OLD DOCTORS

In prehistoric times, people relied on magic and traditional knowledge when they fell ill. But most modern doctors try to use scientific knowledge instead. The first specialist doctors appeared in the time of Ancient Egypt, nearly 5,000 years ago.

Stretched

The Greek doctor Hippocrates (see opposite) invented this device, in which the patient was stretched with ropes tied round their arms and legs. It looks pretty nasty, and it inspired the medieval torture device, the rack. But it was designed to help set broken bones properly – and hospitals still use similar 'traction' devices to relieve pressure on damaged backs.

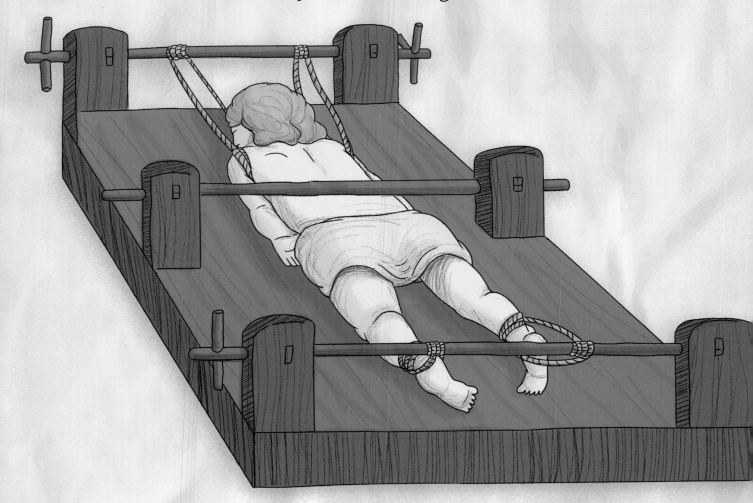

No snakes, please!

Hippocrates lived on the Greek island of Kos 2,500 years ago. Ancient Greek doctors often killed patients by trying to cure them with snake venom, but Hippocrates knew this was wrong – diseases weren't punishments by the gods but had natural causes. He also said doctors had a duty of care to patients.

Doctors today still swear a Hippocratic Oath to treat patients well, based on Hippocrates' ideas.

I want my mummy!

The first known doctor was Imhotep, who lived in Egypt 4,600 years ago. Apparently he could diagnose and treat 200 diseases, such as tuberculosis and arthritis. He knew anatomy, too, and maybe even how blood circulates. He was also a brilliant engineer who built pyramids. So if he didn't cure you, he'd give you a good tomb!

Nasty wound, there! Great!

Galen (about ad 129–200) was the most famous doctor in the Roman Empire. He learned what bodies are really like from the terrible wounds that gladiators suffered in fights. His knowledge became the basis of medicine for the next 1,300 years. Galen boasted: 'I have done as much for medicine as Trajan did for the Roman Empire when he built bridges and roads.'

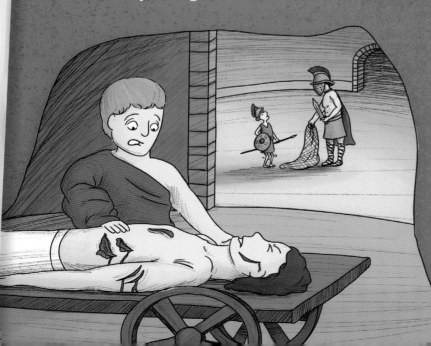

BAD MOODS

In Ancient Greece and Rome and in the Middle Ages, doctors thought you have four body fluids called humours – and you get ill when you have too much of one of them. Their treatments were about trying to put the balance right.

Urine trouble

Some doctors in the Middle Ages thought they could tell what was wrong with you from another body fluid – urine. They didn't just look at its colour. They smelt it, and even tasted it. Uggh! But they knew that a sweet taste meant a patient had diabetes.

Humours and moods

The humours were each linked to different nasty fluids that you sometimes cough up. The humours didn't just affect your body, though. They influenced your whole character. And each was linked to a particular season and type of weather.

A Yellow bile

You may vomit up half-digested food with this yellow stomach juice. Yellow bile was linked to problems with the liver. It was also related to a cross and irritable, or passionate, impulsive nature, and to summer and warm, dry weather.

B Blood

You can sometimes cough up blood or have a nosebleed. Blood was linked to problems with the heart. It was also associated with a cheery and hopeful, optimistic and artistic nature, and to spring and warm, moist weather.

C Phlegm

Phlegm is the slimy stuff you cough up or sneeze out when you have a cold. Phlegm was linked to a shy, reserved, caring and thoughtful – and sometimes lazy – nature, and to winter and cold, wet weather.

D Black bile

Black bile is the smelly liquid you can vomit up even when you haven't eaten. It was linked to problems with the spleen. Black bile was associated with a moody and depressed, but rather analytical nature, and to autumn and cold, dry weather.

A = Hot and Wet

B = Warm and dry

HOT

DRY

WET

COLD

C = Cold and Wet

D = Cold and Dry

BODY BUTCHERS - THE ANATOMISTS

From the 1500s on, people thought it might help to know where things are actually positioned in our bodies (our anatomy) and how they work (our physiology). But finding out could be a rather nasty business!

Burke and Hare

In the early 1800s, criminals often dug up bodies from graves to sell to medical schools. But in Edinburgh in 1828, William Burke and William Hare found a way to speed up the process. They didn't wait for people to die; they just killed them and sold their bodies to Dr Robert Knox for his famous anatomy lectures.

Cut up

In the 1530s, Italian doctor Andreas Vesalius realized that the only way to learn about human anatomy was to cut bodies open. He did this to make detailed, accurate drawings of what is inside. Cutting up bodies is called 'dissection'. In 1543, he dissected the body of a criminal in front of a huge audience.

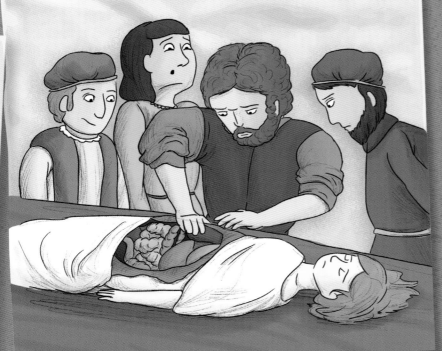

I said half a TEAspoon...

Swiss German doctor Paracelsus (1493–1541) developed the idea that different drugs could be used for different diseases. But he had a strange interest in poisons. When people attacked him for it, he said that poisons are only poisonous if you have a big enough dose. He tested this theory on animals...

Circulation

In the early 1600s, William Harvey showed that blood doesn't just sit in the body, it is pumped round and round by the heart. This was a medical breakthrough. But the way Harvey showed this seems really cruel now. He tied a living dog to a table, then cut it open to show the dog's heart pumping and the blood flowing.

LEECHES AND BLOODLETTING

Next time you complain about having to take medicine when you're ill, just think about what you might have had to go through in the past – anything from being covered in bloodsucking slugs to being cut and made to bleed.

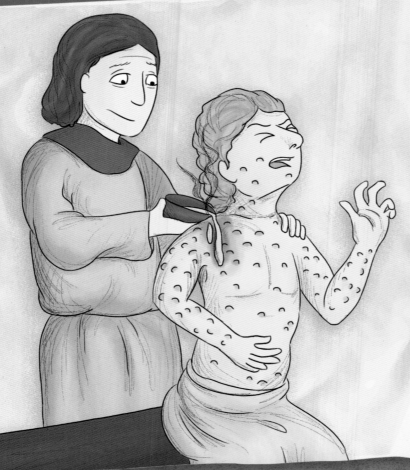

Heavy metal

In the 1490s, the terrible disease syphilis began to spread across Europe. One of its effects was to cover the body in horrible pustules. To treat the disease, doctors spooned the liquid metal mercury on the pustules or made patients sit in a room filled with mercury vapour. But mercury is poisonous and drove patients mad.

Fancy a cup?

Cupping dates back 5,000 years and is still performed by some people today. It involves heating a cup and pressing it hard onto the skin. The heat creates a suction effect that draws blood to the skin under the cup. The extra blood flow is said to reduce pain. But there is little evidence it works.

Blowing smoke up

When Europeans brought tobacco back from America in the 1500s, doctors thought it might help treat some ailments. But some doctors had a strange way of using it. In the 1800s they would light a pipe full of tobacco and use a long tube to blow the smoke up the patient's rear end! They called this a 'tobacco enema'.

You want blood?

In ancient times, many doctors believed having too much blood in your body made you ill. So whenever people fell sick, the doctors would cut open a large blood vessel in the patient's arm or neck to let out blood. Many died or became worse through loss of blood. But the practice went on until the mid-1800s.

Bloodsuckers

You didn't have to cut people to let out blood. Some doctors used leeches to suck it out instead. The great thing about leeches, they thought, is that they can be stuck on close to the diseased organ! Some doctors have recently suggested that leeches might be a good way of treating some ailments after all.

BARBERS AND QUACKS

In the past, there were all kinds of words used to describe doctors – not all of them nice! If you had a bad injury and maybe needed a leg cut off, you'd go to the barber surgeon. If you needed drugs, you could try an apothecary...

Quack pot

The 18th century was the heyday of 'quacks': people who tried to sell you their own brand of medicine – guaranteed to cure your problem! One notorious quack was American Dr Elisha Perkins (1741–99). Perkins claimed he could cure rheumatism and pain by waving two metal rods or 'tractors' over you.

My legs grew back!

Some quacks made absurd promises. A 19th-century cartoon makes fun of the promise of miracle cures made by Morrison's vegetable pills. A man with two wooden legs claims his real legs have grown back, because he's taken Morrison's. The other man is not convinced!

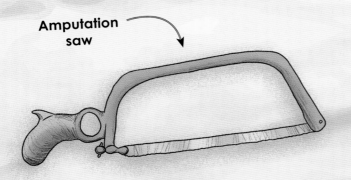

Amputation saw

Sawbones

There was no way to treat a badly injured arm or leg. So the only way to stop the wound going bad and killing you was to remove the wounded part with a saw. The men who did this were called 'sawbones'. Having your leg sawn off was unimaginably painful, since there were no anaesthetics back then.

Barber surgeons

In the Middle Ages, you didn't go to a doctor to have an injured arm or leg amputated – you went to the barber! Barbers were good with knives, so they could cut hair or limbs. They could also cut your arm to let blood. That's why their symbol became a red-and-white pole, representing blood running down an arm.

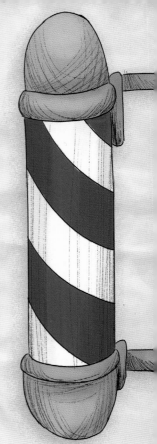

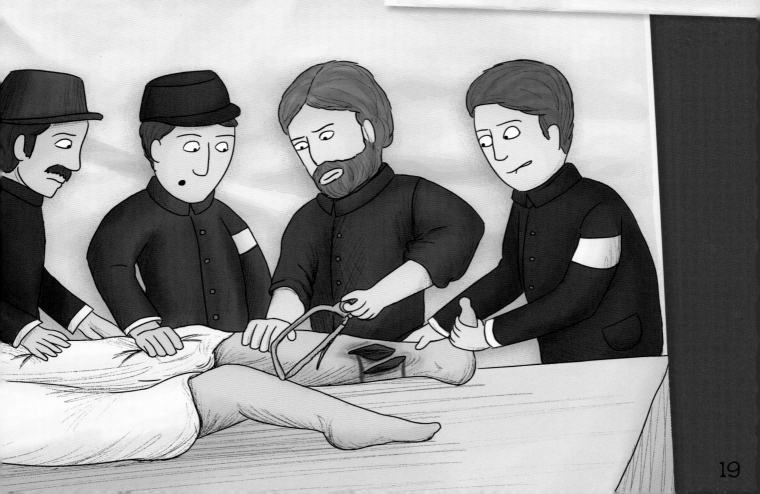

NEW BLOOD

If you lose lots of blood, from an injury or during surgery, your life may be saved by an input of someone else's blood. This is called a 'transfusion'. We now take transfusions for granted, but in the past they could kill you.

Dog to dog

The first ever transfusion was performed on two dogs in 1665 by English physician Richard Lower. He connected an artery in one dog with a vein in the other via a glass pipe. When he sliced an artery in the second dog so that it lost a lot of blood, it was kept alive by blood flowing from the first dog.

Bad blood

No one realized at the time that not all blood is the same. So in 1667, a doctor in Paris, Jean-Baptiste Denys, tried to give a man sheep's blood in the same way Lower had transfused two dogs. But the sheep's blood killed the man. Denys was tried for murder and transfusions were banned.

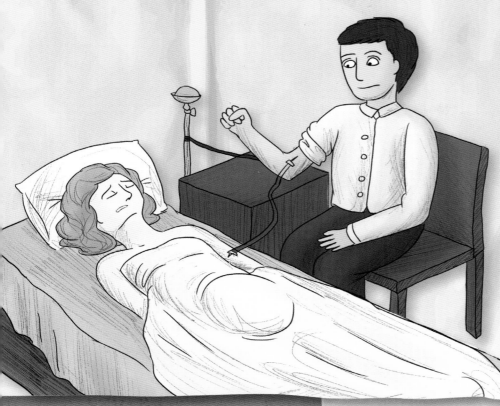

The first human transfusion

In the early 1800s, Dr James Blundell was appalled by how many women died from loss of blood during childbirth. So in 1818, he used a syringe to inject a mother who had lost a lot of blood with blood collected from her husband's arteries. The transfusion worked and the mother survived.

Blood types

Blundell's success was a lucky one-off, and most transfusions performed afterwards killed the patient. Then in 1900 Austrian-American doctor Karl Landsteiner (1868–1943) realized why. Blood belongs to three different groups – A, B and O – and for a transfusion to work, the blood must be of the right kind.

Blood bank

The first transfusions were made by hooking the donor up directly to the patient. But then it was discovered that blood could be stored for several days in a refrigerator. In World War I, stores of blood called blood banks were set up, saving the lives of the countless wounded soldiers.

SICK HOSPITALS

The first proper hospitals appeared in India some 2,400 years ago and cared for the sick very well. But sometimes in the past, hospitals were horrible places as likely to kill you as cure you.

Holy hospitals!

Some of the first hospitals in Europe were in nunneries. But they could be terrible places where you might pray to get out alive. In the infamous Hôtel-Dieu in Paris in the 18th century, several people would be crammed into each bed, and patients with infectious diseases mixed with the mentally ill. Very few survived.

Lady with the Lamp

Nurse Florence Nightingale was shocked by the crowded, dirty conditions in field hospitals for British soldiers wounded in the Crimean War in the 1850s. Her insistence on sanitary conditions, and taking close personal care of patients – even at night – helped change hospitals from places where people went to die to places of healing.

Bedlam!

Set up in 1247, the Bethlehem hospital in London was the first hospital for the mentally ill in Europe. But it was once a house of horrors, where distressed patients were chained up in appalling conditions. Their wailing was so horrific that the hospital's nickname, 'Bedlam', came to mean dreadful noise and chaos.

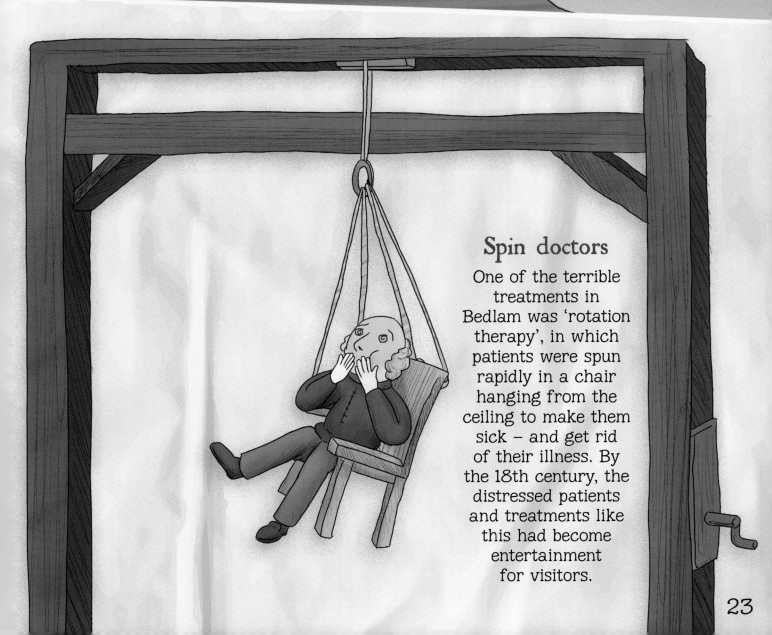

Spin doctors

One of the terrible treatments in Bedlam was 'rotation therapy', in which patients were spun rapidly in a chair hanging from the ceiling to make them sick – and get rid of their illness. By the 18th century, the distressed patients and treatments like this had become entertainment for visitors.

TAKING THE PUSTULE

Your body can be protected against disease by deliberately infecting it with germs. The germs prime your body's defences, or 'immune system', to fight the disease. This is called 'inoculation'.

Here, have some germs!

The Chinese found how to inoculate against the terrible disease smallpox 1,000 years ago. They took pus-filled scabs from smallpox victims, dried and powdered them, then blew the powder up people's noses through a tube. Some died from the germs, but many more became immune to the disease.

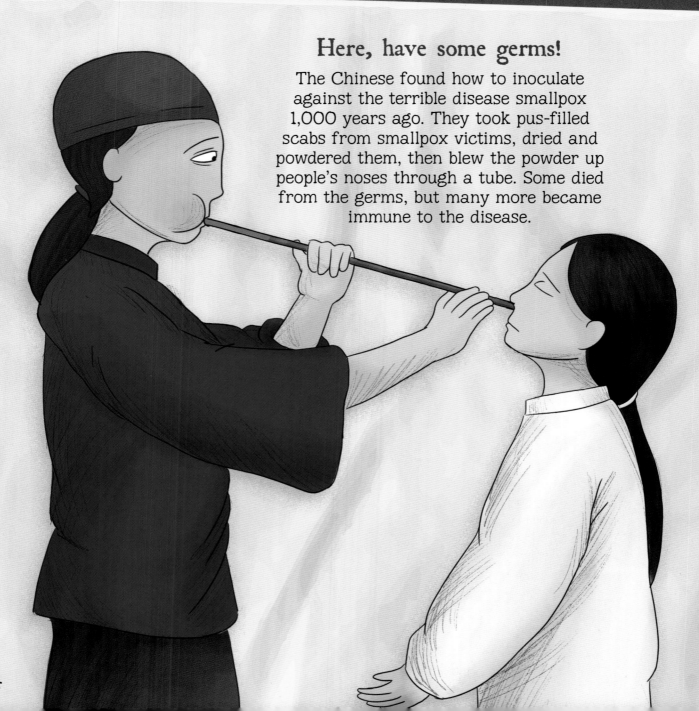

Beautiful milkmaids

In the 1700s, even those who survived smallpox were left badly scarred by the pustules. Yet milkmaids were famed for their flawless complexions. When they milked cows, it seems, they caught a mild form of the disease called cowpox and this made them immune to smallpox.

Inoculation in America

Smallpox once killed many Americans. But in 1706, Boston's Reverend Cotton Mather learned about inoculation from his African slave Onesimus. Later, in 1721, Mather persuaded local doctor Zabdiel Boylston to try inoculation in Boston. Many Bostonians objected that this was interfering with God's will, but the trials proved a success.

Vaccination

Inoculation with smallpox germs was dangerous. English doctor Edward Jenner wondered if cowpox germs might safely give the same protection. So in 1796, he injected cowpox pus into eight-year-old James Phipps. Luckily for James, it worked. Using mild forms of germs for inoculation is called 'vaccination'. By 1979, smallpox had been entirely eradicated from the world in this way.

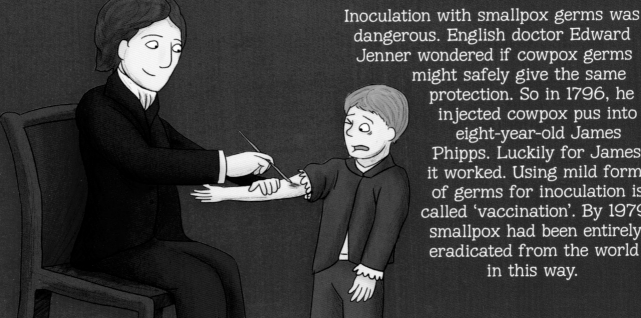

CAN'T FEEL A THING

Without anaesthetics, major operations such as heart surgery would be impossible. Anaesthetics are chemicals that send you to sleep (general anaesthetic) or dull the pain in the affected area (local anaesthetic), while surgery is performed.

Sleepover

In 1847, Scottish doctor James Simpson had a party and tried out another anaesthetic, chloroform, on two of his doctor friends. It knocked all three of them out. Soon chloroform was being widely used for anaesthetizing patients for operations. Then it was realized chloroform is slightly poisonous.

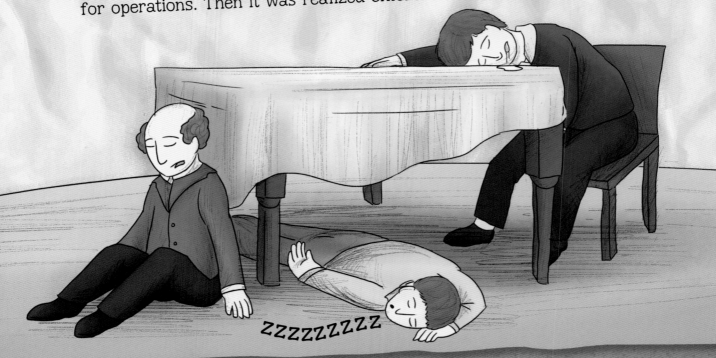

ZZZZZZZZZ

It's a knockout

In Massachusetts in 1846, American dentist William Morton pulled a tooth out while his patient was fast asleep. This was the first ever successful operation under general anaesthetic. The anaesthetic he used was a chemical called 'ether', which was warmed in a jar to create vapours that the patient breathed in.

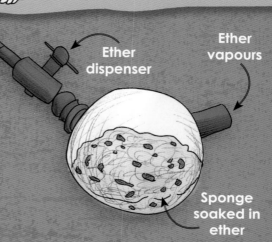

Ether dispenser

Ether vapours

Sponge soaked in ether

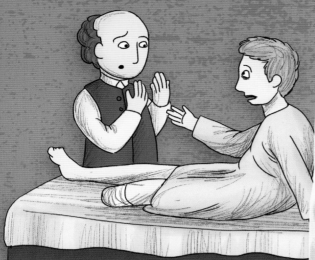

What a laugh!

In the 1830s, people went to demonstrations of the effects of nitrous oxide, known as 'laughing gas' because it makes you laugh and feel pain less. In 1844, dentist Horace Wells made patients breathe laughing gas from a pig's bladder and then painlessly pulled teeth out. But other dentists found patients cried out in pain midway through.

When are you going to begin?

Just a few months after Morton's tooth extraction, Scottish surgeon Robert Liston amputated a patient's leg while he was entirely unconscious from ether. The patient came round, entirely unaware the operation had been performed, asking Liston, 'When are you going to begin?'

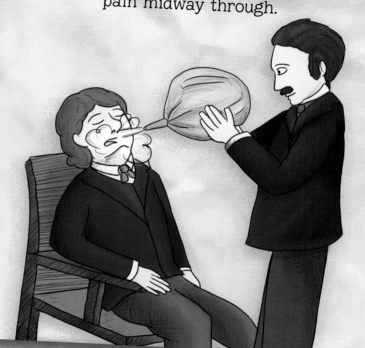

Dangerous darts

Some native South American people blow poison darts dipped in a plant extract called 'curare'. Curare paralyses victims so completely that they stop breathing and die. In the past, curare was tried as a general anaesthetic – until it was realized that although it made patients immobile, they could still feel the pain of an operation!

MEDICAL TIMES

Despite the sometimes odd treatments from the past, medical practice has made great progress through time. Here are some of the milestones.

3000 BCE

100 AC

420 BC Science not magic

Greek doctor Hippocrates insisted that diseases have natural causes. He also insisted that doctors took an oath to treat patients properly. It is called the Hippocratic Oath, and doctors still take it today.

3,000 BCE Old herbalists

In India, the Ayurvedic system of herbal medicine dates back 5,000 years and is still practised today.

2,600 BC The first doctor

The first doctor whose name we know was Imhotep, who lived in Ancient Egypt. He was also a priest and an engineer, and was worshipped as a god.

About AD 200 Studying the body

Learning about the body from studying sheep and gladiator's wounds, Roman doctor Galen wrote a textbook that became the main guide for doctors for the next 1,300 years.

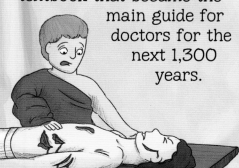

1818 New blood

Dr James Blundell made the first successful blood transfusion to save a woman from dying in childbirth. Now blood transfusions save hundreds of thousands of lives every year.

1967 Heart transplant

South African surgeon Christiaan Barnard performed the first human heart transplant, taking a healthy heart from someone who had recently died and swapping it for the failing heart of a patient.

About 1030 Medical textbook

Muslim scholar Avicenna's *Canon of Medicine* became the standard medical textbook for the next 700 years.

1900

1400

1543 Human anatomy

Italian Andreas Vesalius was the first to realize that to find out about human anatomy – what goes on inside the human body – you have to cut up real dead bodies.

1846 Sleeping through it

American dentist William Morton performed the first operation under general anaesthetic when he sent his patient to sleep with ether fumes while he pulled a tooth out.

zzzzzzzzz

DOCTORS MAKE ME SICK!

The Ancient Egyptians thought they could cure toothache by slitting open the belly of a mouse and laying its still-warm body on your gums. Uggh!

In the past, doctors stopped severe bleeding, perhaps after an amputation, by cauterizing the wound – scorching it with red-hot metal or boiling tar. Aaagh!!!

In 1738, the British parliament paid quack Joanna Stephens £3,000 for her bladder stone cure, and the Prime Minister Robert Walpole ate 80 kg (175 lb) of it – but it was just soap and eggshells. Frothy!

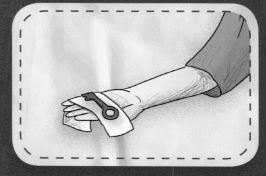

If you were bitten by a dog with rabies, a priest might scorch the bite with a red-hot key or nail, called St Hubert's Key. Surprisingly it could actually work if done soon after the bite, by killing the virus. Ouch!

In the Middle Ages, if a doctor offered you a clyster to treat your illness, run. A clyster was a tube that he stuck up your bottom and then poured in hot water, or pig's bile. Eeeegh!

To cure a sore throat in the Middle Ages, a doctor might tell you to eat dog poo. No need to eat it wet – dried and mixed with honey was fine... Mmm!

GLOSSARY

Amputation	Cutting off a limb
Anaesthetic	A chemical that numbs pain or sends you to sleep
Bile	A dark green fluid made by the liver, and a passionate, impulsive humour
Bloodletting	Cutting the skin to let out blood in the vain hope of curing illness
Cupping	Applying heated cups to the skin to draw the blood to the surface
Diabetes	A disease caused by fluctuations in sugar levels in the blood
Enema	The injection of fluid or gas into the bottom for medical purposes
Grafting	Attaching tissue from someone else, or from another part of your own body
Humour	One of four states of the body that old medical theory believed needed to be in balance to maintain good health
Immune system	The body's own microscopic defences against germs
Inoculation	Using germs to stimulate the immune system to guard against infection
Phlegm	The slimy stuff produced when you have a cold, and a shy, reserved humour
Transfusion	Transferring blood from one person to another
Transplant	Replacing one person's faulty body organs with another's healthy organs
Vaccination	Using dead or inactivated germs to stimulate the body's immune system to guard against infection

Index

A
anaesthetics 26, 27, 29
anatomy 14, 15, 29

B
barber surgeons 19
Bedlam 23
black bile 12, 13
blood 12, 13
    letting 17, 19
    transfusions 20, 21, 29
broken bones 10

C
chloroform 26
circulation 15
cupping 16
curare 27

D
dentist 27
dissection 15
doctors 6, 7, 10, 11, 30, 31

E
ether 26, 27

G
Galen 11, 28

H
Hippocratic Oath 11, 28
hospitals 22, 23
humours 12, 13

I
Imhotep 11, 28
inoculations 24, 25

L
laughing gas 27
leeches 17

M
mercury 16

N
Nightingale, Florence 22
nose jobs 9

P
phlegm 12, 13
poisons 15, 16, 27

Q
quacks 18

S
sawbones 19
smallpox 24, 25
stitches 8
surgeons 8, 9, 19

T
timeline 28, 29
tobacco enemas 17
transplants 9, 29
trepanning 8

U
urine 12

V
vaccinations 25

Y
yellow bile 12, 13

The Author

John Farndon is the author of many books on science, technology and nature, including the international best-sellers *Do Not Open* and *Do You Think You're Clever?* He has been shortlisted five times for the Royal Society's Young People's Book Prize for a science book.

The Illustrator

Venitia Dean grew up in Brighton, UK. She has loved drawing ever since she could hold a pencil. After receiving a digital drawing tablet for her 19th birthday she transferred to working digitally. She hasn't looked back since!